A souvenir guide

Saltram

Devon

National Trust

Origins and Owners

The name of the estate originates from the salt harvested from the nearby estuary. Salt was a vital commodity in the Middle Ages and consequently Saltram gained early status. On this, later owners built their fortunes and ultimately an impressive Georgian mansion house that was transferred to the National Trust in 1957.

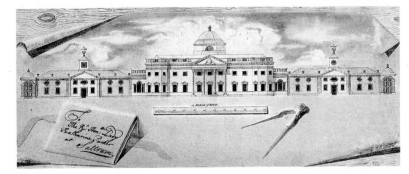

The Bagges

It is known that Sir James Bagge bought the farm at Saltram in 1614. As the Collector of Customs for Plymouth and Fowey, MP for and briefly Mayor of Plymouth, he wielded a great deal of local power. Unscrupulous and curmudgeonly, he was nevertheless almost saintly compared to his son, also called James, who inherited the estate in 1624.

The son was apparently 'prepared to go to almost any length in his quest for personal power and wealth'. The younger James was closely allied to King James I's favourite, the Duke of Buckingham, who often stayed at Saltram. On Charles I's accession, Buckingham persuaded the King to launch an attack on the Spanish at Cadiz, and Bagge was appointed prestmaster (in charge of press ganging reluctant sailors) and victualler (responsible for provisions) for the expedition. Despite being knighted by Charles I, Bagge audaciously embezzled £55,000 by supplying the fleet with rotten food that 'killed four thousand of the King's Subjects'. For unknown reasons, the King defended Bagge, but when a second embezzlement charge was levelled, Archbishop Laud stated, 'I have now done with that bottomless bag.'

Bagge died in debt and disgrace in 1638. Most of his property was seized by the throne, but Saltram passed to his son George. According to an illustrated map of 1643, by this point the house was a three-storey building with a hipped roof and two large gables. It appears to have been constructed around a central courtyard, which still survives at the heart of present-day Saltram (see page 55).

Bagges to Parkers

This much-coveted house became an important bargaining chip in the seething politics of the 17th century. George Bagge was the Deputy Governor of Plymouth and a Royalist who, finding himself on the losing side at the end of the Civil War in 1651, had to pay the Commonwealth Government £582 or forfeit the estate. In 1660 Saltram passed to Captain Henry Hatsell, a Parliamentarian, but on the Restoration of Charles II, the estate was handed to Sir George Carteret as a reward for loaning the King a very large sum during the Civil War.

In 1712, Saltram was bought by George Parker, an affluent country squire from nearby Boringdon. George let the house to tenants during his lifetime and left it to his son, John, on his death in 1743.

Above Lady Catherine's unrealised commission, possibly by William Kent, for a new house at Boringdon or Saltram (East Corridor)

Below Saltram's 18th-century Palladian (inspired by 16th-century architect Andrea Palladio) façade was added to the Tudor mansion by John Parker and Lady Catherine

Opposite Saltram derives its name from the salt extracted from the Plym Estuary

The Parkers

Owners are in CAPITALS
Asterisk denotes portrait in the house

John Parker I (1703–68)

John Parker II (1734/5–88)

John Parker III (1772–1840)

Edmund (1810–64)

Edmund (1877–1951)

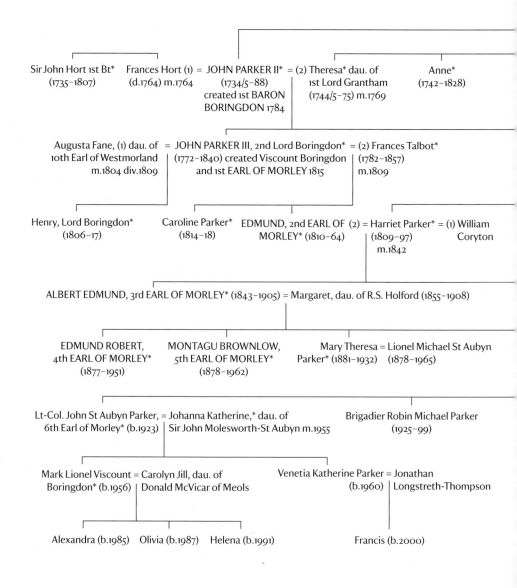

Sir John Hort 1st Bt* (1735–1807) — Frances Hort (1) (d.1764) m.1764 = JOHN PARKER II* (1734/5–88) created 1st BARON BORINGDON 1784 = (2) Theresa* dau. of 1st Lord Grantham (1744/5–75) m.1769 — Anne* (1742–1828)

Augusta Fane, (1) dau. of 10th Earl of Westmorland m.1804 div.1809 = JOHN PARKER III, 2nd Lord Boringdon* (1772–1840) created Viscount Boringdon and 1st EARL OF MORLEY 1815 = (2) Frances Talbot* (1782–1857) m.1809

Henry, Lord Boringdon* (1806–17)   Caroline Parker* (1814–18)   EDMUND, 2nd EARL OF MORLEY* (1810–64) (2) = Harriet Parker* (1809–97) m.1842 = (1) William Coryton

ALBERT EDMUND, 3rd EARL OF MORLEY* (1843–1905) = Margaret, dau. of R.S. Holford (1855–1908)

EDMUND ROBERT, 4th EARL OF MORLEY* (1877–1951)   MONTAGU BROWNLOW, 5th EARL OF MORLEY* (1878–1962)   Mary Theresa Parker* (1881–1932) = Lionel Michael St Aubyn (1878–1965)

Lt-Col. John St Aubyn Parker, 6th Earl of Morley* (b.1923) = Johanna Katherine,* dau. of Sir John Molesworth-St Aubyn m.1955   Brigadier Robin Michael Parker (1925–99)

Mark Lionel Viscount Boringdon* (b.1956) = Carolyn Jill, dau. of Donald McVicar of Meols   Venetia Katherine Parker (b.1960) = Jonathan Longstreth-Thompson

Alexandra (b.1985)   Olivia (b.1987)   Helena (b.1991)   Francis (b.2000)

Elizabeth Fowell (1) = GEORGE PARKER = (2) Anne Buller
(d.1743)

JOHN PARKER* = Catherine, dau. of 1st Earl Poulett*
(1703–68) m.1725 | (1706–58)

Thomas, 2nd Lord
Grantham*
(1738–86)

Frederick*
('Fritz') (1746–92)

Henrietta
(d.1808)

Montagu Edmund = Charity* dau. of
Parker of Whiteway* | Admiral Paul Ourry*
(1737–1813) m.1775 | (1752–86)

Theresa Parker* = Hon. George
(1775–1856)   Villiers

Montagu E. Parker* = Harriet
(1778–1831) | Newcombe

Montagu E. Newcombe Parker
(1807–58)

Katherine Parker* (d.1910)

John Holford Parker = Marjory Katharine Elizabeth St Aubyn
(1886–1955) | (1893–1987), dau. of 2nd Baron St Levan

Nigel Geoffrey Parker = Georgina Jane, dau. of
(b.1931) | Sir Thomas Gordon Devitt, 2nd Bt

Edward Geoffrey Parker = Alice Elliot
(b.1967)

Theresa Hilaria Parker = Simon Latham
(b.1966)

Cordelia (b.1994)   Oliver (b.1996)   Henry (b.1997)   Thomas (b.2000)   Toby (b.1995)

Lady Catherine (1706–58)

Theresa (1744/5–75)

Frances Talbot (1782–1857)

Albert (1843–1905)

Montagu (1878–1962)

The Parkers

The Parkers were an ambitious family. They served their country in the houses of Parliament, in the royal court and on the battlefields of the Boer Wars. Some made money, others married money and several were very adept at spending money.

John Parker I

John Parker married Lady Catherine Poulett, daughter of the 1st Earl Poulett, Secretary of State to Queen Anne, in 1725 and after some initial uncertainty about where they were to live, he supported his wife's ambitious plans to expand Saltram. A design was commissioned either from William Kent (see page 3), the leading Palladian architect of the day, or a member of his circle, but was not executed. Instead, possibly for reasons of economy, an unknown architect was commissioned to design three classical façades. Each façade was different, and they were added to the much older existing buildings, with little attention paid to making the internal layout correspond with the exterior.

No expense was spared on the interior; the plasterwork and joinery in the main rooms were superb, with some of the best craftsmen of the age employed.

John Parker II

John Parker II, Baron Boringdon, was the well-connected, educated eldest son of a wealthy landowner and was returned as MP for first Bodmin and then Devon while still in his twenties. His main interests were shooting, horse-racing and gambling. In 1764 he married Frances Hort, a cousin of Lord Shelburne, later Prime Minister. The couple undertook a trip to Italy, but his young bride fell ill and died in Naples. In 1769 he married again. Marriage to the Hon. Theresa Robinson, daughter of the 1st Lord Grantham, brought him increased social status. Theresa threw herself into the remodelling of Saltram with enthusiasm. Cultured and cosmopolitan, she played an active part in many aspects of the improvements at Saltram.

In 1768, the year he inherited Saltram, John commissioned the multi-talented architect and designer Robert Adam to create two new rooms in the house. John and Theresa furnished these and other rooms with the best of work of contemporary artists and craftsmen.

A royal visit
In August 1789, George III, Queen Charlotte and their retinue, including Frances 'Fanny' Burney (above), later Madame D'Arblay, Mistress of the Robes to the Queen, came to stay at Saltram during the Royal Household's visit to the West Country.

'The house is one of the most magnificent in the kingdom. It accommodated us all, even to every footman … the state apartments on the ground floor are superb; hung with crimson damask and ornamented with pictures…. Its view is noble; it extends to Plymouth, Mount Edgecumbe, and the neighbouring fine country. The sea at times fills up a part of the domain almost close to the house, and then its prospect is complete.'

From the diary and letters of
Madame D'Arblay, 1789–93

John Parker III, 1st Earl of Morley

John was a handsome and well-connected Tory MP, progressive in outlook. He supported Catholic emancipation, parliamentary reform and vaccination against smallpox. He was created Viscount Boringdon and Earl of Morley in 1815. He had one child with his first wife, Lady Augusta Fane, and two with his second wife Frances Talbot, but he also acknowledged the three children from his long liaison with Lady Elizabeth Monck, all of whom lived with him on the estate. One, Augustus Stapleton, even features in a painting by Nicholas Condy of the Library, from where estate affairs were conducted.

John employed John Foulston, the architect of Regency Plymouth, to extend the Library and to design a new entrance in the Greek Revival style. John was also partial to ambitious engineering projects, reclaiming marshland at Saltram, which later became a racecourse, and throwing a cast-iron bridge across the Laira (see page 22). On his death in 1840, he left a quarter of a million pounds' worth of debt to his heir, Edmund.

Above The Library; by Nicholas Condy, c.1825. From left to right: 1st Earl of Morley; Augustus Stapleton, his son by Lady Elizabeth Monck; Catchpole the butler; his second wife, Frances; and their son, Edmund (private collection)

Edmund Parker, 2nd Earl of Morley

Edmund was described by his son Albert as a tall, amiable man. He was Gentleman in Waiting to Queen Victoria. Sadly he suffered a stroke that left him paralysed down his right side, which forced him to give up public life. Albert was convinced that his father's health problems were brought about by the huge debt that he inherited. Edmund was not a competent businessman and succeeded only in increasing the debt. His half-brother Augustus helped him in his efforts to extricate the family from debt. In 1861 he took the decision that saved Saltram from being sold: he let the house to a tenant and took his family to live abroad with relatives. He was never to return to Satram, suffering a second and fatal stroke in 1864.

Above Edmund, 2nd Earl of Morley; by Frederick Say, c.1830–40 (Sitting Room)

Opposite left 3rd Earl of Morley's wife and son, by Ellis Roberts, c.1890 (Sitting Room)

Opposite right Albert, 3rd Earl of Morley; by Ellis Roberts, c.1890 (Sitting Room)

Albert Edmund Parker, 3rd Earl of Morley

Albert, a brilliant academic, sat on the Liberal benches in the House of Lords and had a distinguished political career, serving as Under-Secretary of State for War from 1880 to 1885 and Deputy Speaker from 1889 to 1905.

Following a judicious marriage to the daughter of Robert Stayner Holford, an extremely wealthy businessman and the creator of Westonbirt and its famous arboretum, Albert was able to begin tackling the inherited burden of debt. At the age of 41 he returned with his family to Saltram, where he began a major programme of repairs and improvements, funded by selling the Laira Bridge and a number of paintings by Sir Joshua Reynolds and Anthony Van Dyck. He spent £16,000 on drainage and building, and put his father-in-law's expertise to good use in the garden. Saltram entered a late Victorian golden age.

Edmund Robert Parker, 4th Earl of Morley

Money worries continued into the 20th century. The cost of running the estate was outstripping income, and farm rents were still low due to the agricultural depression.

Salvation for Saltram came when Edmund inherited Westonbirt in Gloucestershire and Dorchester House in central London from his mother. The London house was sold and promptly demolished to create the Dorchester Hotel. The revenue generated, according to *Country Life* in 1926, '...maintains this fine 18th-century house and its priceless contents with exact care and informed judgment'.

Far left Edmund Parker, 4th Earl of Morley

Left The Red Drawing Room at Dorchester House. The house was demolished in 1929

Below The garden front of Westonbirt

Fund in lieu of death duties in 1957. Lady Astor, former MP for Plymouth and doyenne of Cliveden, suggested that Saltram should be given to the National Trust, which it was 18 months later. Monty retained a lease of the house for his lifetime, and the Trust began the long and painstaking business of conserving and caring for this remarkable property.

Saltram is now funded by the National Trust, assisted by income generated by visitors, and helped by annual grants from English Heritage.

Left A hero's welcome for Montagu Parker on his return from the Boer War in 1902

Below Montagu Parker, later 5th Earl of Morley

Montagu Brownlow Parker, 5th Earl of Morley

Montagu was a veteran of the Boer War and a hero of the First World War, mentioned in dispatches five times and recipient of the Croix de Guerre.

Briefly an archaeologist, Monty was convinced that the Ark of the Covenant was buried beneath the Temple of Jerusalem, and in 1909 he joined an expedition to unearth it. The team reached the Mosque of Omar and bribed a sheikh to allow them in, but the sheikh's brother exposed the plan when Monty's team refused to pay. Uproar ensued and the archaeologists were lucky to escape with their lives.

Inheriting Saltram in 1951 at the age of 73, Monty endeavoured to deal with the enormous backlog of repairs, but struggled to meet the death duties on the estate. The enormous kitchen garden was let, but it was apparent that radical action was needed. He decided to transfer the house, its contents and 291 acres of park to H.M. Treasury, via the National Land

The women of Saltram

The Parker family had a happy knack of marrying money just at the moment when it was most needed. The women who 'married in' were partners in every sense, fully involved in developing the estate and shaping the way it looked and was used.

Lady Catherine Poulett

In 1725, John Parker made a very good match by marrying Catherine Poulett, daughter of the 1st Earl Poulett. Lady Catherine brought with her a fortune, sophisticated taste and a great deal of energy. She was responsible for creating much of Saltram as we now see it.

The Parkers commissioned a design from architect William Kent or a member of his circle, but baulked at its grand scale. Instead, they employed a West Country architect to make more modest changes to the exterior, saving their money for the interiors.

The exterior of the Tudor manor house was transformed by adding new south, east and west wings. As for the interiors, the stucco ceiling, the Italian panels over the doorways and the carved stone chimneypiece in the Entrance Hall were typical of the high quality of work Lady Catherine demanded. She was almost certainly responsible for introducing Chinese wallpapers, the height of fashion, costing up to seven shillings a yard – what the average Devon workman might earn in a week.

Lady Catherine was instrumental in forging the Parker family's enduring and close relationship with the painter Sir Joshua Reynolds,

Above Lady Catherine Parker, whose money helped to pay for the rebuilding of Saltram in the 1740s; attributed to Michael Dahl (Staircase Hall)

Left The Chinese mirror paintings were introduced by John and Lady Catherine Parker

Opposite Theresa Parker; by Sir Joshua Reynolds, 1770–72 (detail) (Saloon)

who was born in the nearby parish of Plympton St Maurice in 1723.

Lady Catherine died in 1758 and her husband a decade later, leaving unfinished his commission for the Saloon. More than £32,000 was found hidden about the house after John Parker's death, providing the means for his son to continue embellishing Saltram in some style.

Theresa Robinson

Theresa Robinson was the daughter of the 1st Lord Grantham and goddaughter of the Empress Maria Theresa of Austria, the mother of Marie Antoinette. Through this marriage John Parker II advanced up the social scale and in 1784 was created Baron Boringdon.

Theresa came from a well-travelled, cosmopolitan background and was a gifted artist and designer. She was much involved in all the improvements, including selecting the works of art and furnishings. She had help from her brother Thomas, who was living in Madrid at the time, asking him to keep an eye out for furnishings for her new home.

John Parker II was MP for Bodmin, and the couple divided their time between London and Devon, where John threw himself avidly into the country pursuits of shooting and horse-racing. Theresa fell ill shortly after the birth of their daughter in 1775 and died aged only 31. Joshua Reynolds wrote that she 'seemed to possess by a kind of intuition that propriety of taste and right thinking which others but imperfectly acquire by long labour and application'.

'Remember that if you meet with anything abroad, of pictures, bronzes etc that is valuable in itself, beautiful and proper for any part of Saltram … you must not lose an opportunity of procuring it for us.'

Theresa in a letter to her brother
Thomas in Madrid

Anne Robinson

After Theresa's sudden death her elder sister Anne Robinson (or Aunt Nanny) came to Saltram to look after her small nephew and niece. She also acted as hostess for her brother-in-law and oversaw the running of the household and estate.

Anne never married; there are contemporary descriptions which suggest she was rather dry and humourless. She devoted her life to looking after her sister's children and her brother-in-law, particular during his last illness. John Parker II acknowledged her contribution to his family in his will, leaving her 500 guineas, all his wine, his carriages, a silver inkwell and a pocket watch.

Saltram provided her with a home and an outlet for her love of the countryside, gardening, needlework and her organisational skills. She stayed for 20 years, even after the death of Lord Boringdon in 1788, until her nephew came of age and was able to take over the estate. She eventually took a house in Park Street in London where she died in 1828.

Frances Talbot

John Parker III was circumspect about remarrying. He had previously been married to Lady Augusta Fane, the daughter of the Earl of Westmoreland in 1804, but her elopement with Sir Arthur Paget five years later caused a great scandal and he divorced her.

In 1809 he married Miss Frances Talbot, the daughter of a Norfolk surgeon known in society for her ready wit and gaiety along with her skill as an amateur artist. She was, nevertheless, a rather surprising choice in that she had no title that might bring advancement and certainly no fortune to help reduce the family debt.

She did, however, have a seemingly endless capacity for forgiveness. She accepted as her own not only her stepson Henry, but also the three illegitimate sons from her husband's long liaison with Lady Elizabeth Monck.

Her happy contented personality drew friends around her; she was always welcome at balls and parties. Not afraid to mildly shock her neighbours, she introduced them to waltzing and entertained them with her laughter and spontaneity.

Unfortunately she experienced poor health and suffered at the hands of the many remedies prescribed for her. Three miscarriages and two full-term pregnancies were borne with her customary stoicism. She outlived her husband by 17 years, occupying herself with painting and writing and maintaining a lively interest in society and world events. Her death came suddenly in 1857. She was a truly remarkable lady who had come from quiet country society in Norfolk to embrace life amongst the aristocracy, respected and admired by all who knew her.

Above Frances Talbot; by Thomas Phillips, 1802

Left The Hon. Anne Robinson, sister of the 1st Baron Boringdon's 2nd wife, Theresa (Sitting Room)

Opposite John Parker III (aged nine) and his sister Theresa (four); by Sir Joshua Reynolds, 1779. When their mother died shortly after Theresa's birth, Anne Robinson came to Saltram to look after them and their father (Red Room)

The Parkers as patrons

In the 18th century Saltram was a melting pot of creative activity, and it is certain that what the Parker family lacked in funds, they more than made up for in matters of taste and patronage.

Robert Adam

John Parker II commissioned Robert Adam to design two rooms of the house. By the late 1760s, Adam was the most fashionable architect in Britain, and greatly in demand. His Neo-classical schemes were based on his minute personal observations of antique buildings and ancient survivals around the Mediterranean, but leavened with his own

Above Giltwood armchairs in the Saloon, attributed to Thomas Chippendale

Left Robert Adam's design for the east wall of the Saloon, 1768 (East Corridor)

lightness of touch and acuteness of detail. Robert Adam's unique vision involved complex pastel colour schemes, softer and more decorative surfaces, and an early example of total design. Adam designed every aspect of each scheme for which he was commissioned, from ceilings to carpets, side tables to settees, door handles to firedogs. Some of his minutely detailed plans for Saltram survive to this day in the house and in the Soane Museum in London.

Sir Joshua Reynolds

From relatively modest beginnings, Sir Joshua Reynolds became one of Britain's finest and most fashionable portrait painters and was the first President of the Royal Academy. He was a frequent visitor to Saltram, as he was particularly friendly with Theresa, and he is believed to have advised the family on buying pictures by other artists. There are eleven portraits by him at Saltram. In addition there is a touchingly affectionate and informal portrait of the artist himself, painted by his protégée and friend, Angelica Kauffman.

Leading artists and manufacturers

The Parkers had keenly fashionable tastes and as a result Saltram is a microcosm of the very best of late 18th-century fine and decorative arts. There are paintings by Sir Peter Paul Rubens, Angelica Kauffman and Sir Joshua Reynolds, copies of Old Master paintings, furniture from Thomas Chippendale, the most exquisite chinoiserie, oriental ceramics and wallpaper, and the latest products of Josiah Wedgwood.

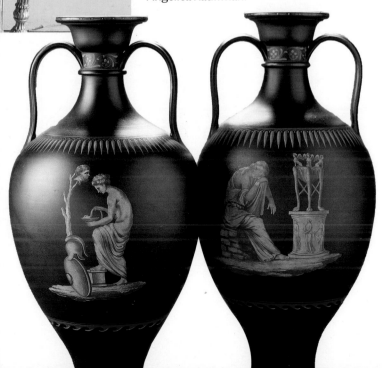

Above *Portrait of the artist*; by Sir Joshua Reynolds, 1767 (Staircase Hall)

Left A pair of black basalt ware vases in the Library, believed to be by Wedgwood & Bentley, 1770–75

Saltram is located on a natural peninsula between the Laira, as the Plym Estuary is known, and Chelson Creek. From the estate, visitors can look south and west across Plymouth Sound to Cornwall. Plymouth is close at hand and Saltram offers all who visit an escape from urban living.

Until the late 18th century the main access was via a tidal crossing, from Crabtree to Blaxton Point. By building an embankment across Plympton marshes in 1770, to the north of the house, Lord Boringdon created a more formal approach to the park, adding a lodge which is now lost.

In 1772, Robert Adam designed a pair of lodges for a site close to the alternative main entrance to the park at Merafield. Two cubic gatehouses in the classical style and a lodge-keeper's cottage added gravitas to the entrance to the estate, particularly at night when the gates were illuminated by flaming braziers.

The lodges were moved to their present location at the eastern end of the park by the 1st Earl, and were restored by the National Trust in 1961.

The Amphitheatre

Below Saltram Wood, on the banks of the Laira, is the Amphitheatre, believed to have been built before 1743. This Neo-classical structure, a whimsical folly, was designed as the perfect addition to an idealised landscape, and was portrayed in this way by William Tomkins in 1770. Visible even today from the opposite bank, the Amphitheatre would greatly have impressed visitors arriving by boat.

The Amphitheatre was cut into the rock, and has three arches. Originally it was roofed and there were four vases along the top of the three-arched structure, with masks below each arch; steps lined with vases lead down to a lawn jutting into the estuary. The centrepiece of the grassy apron was a large bronze statue of a gladiator, but that was stolen in 1817, supposedly by bargemen.

Much of the landscape seen from the house was influenced by the designs of Nathaniel Richmond, the London-based landscape architect who worked with Lancelot 'Capability' Brown in his younger days. He is recorded as working at Saltram from 1767 until 1774, during which time Theresa Parker commented upon his slow progress. But he did draw up the designs for the Orangery, which was erected under the supervision of Henry Stockman (see page 30).

Opposite A woodland track on the Saltram estate

Below left The Plym Estuary seen through one of the arches of the Amphitheatre

Below right *The Amphitheatre at Saltram*, 1770; by William Tomkins (Garden Room)

Saltram as a working estate

The estate was always run as a commercial entity and for centuries it both supported the Parker family in some style and provided a living for hundreds of their servants and employees. At its peak, the estate consisted of 4,000 acres; today 500 acres remain in the care of the National Trust.

To the north, the Parkers allowed the ancient woodland to survive, but to the south they converted the land to agricultural use, growing corn and other crops. Deer were introduced for hunting, but these had declined by the early 19th century. Agriculture remained the main source of revenue and a number of farms on the estate were leased out. Saltram Home Farm was located on the edge of Chelson Meadow. The farm was compulsorily purchased by Plymouth City Council in the 1950s, but the farmer's family still grazes cattle on the site.

Timber was always a lucrative source of income, supplying the shipyards and barrel makers of Plymouth. Saltram had its own team of foresters, a sawpit and mill to process timber. More than 40,000 trees were planted on the estate in the 18th century.

Below *Saltram from the North East*; by Philip Hutchings Rogers

Horse breeding and racing

The stable block was first erected in the 1740s by John and Lady Catherine Parker; the coach-house range was added in the 1760s, and a cupola and turret clock were added to the earlier buildings by John Parker II.

John Parker II was a turf enthusiast and was often to be found at Newmarket and Epsom, no easy journey from Plymouth. His horse 'Saltram' won the Derby in 1783. He was a keen horse-breeder, and established a well-regarded racing stud at Newmarket; indeed, several of his horses were bought by the Prince of Wales.

In 1806/7 his son John Parker III built an embankment to the south-west of the house to reclaim land from the River Plym. This improvement cost £15,000, a fortune for the time, and entailed mortgaging Saltram. In 1828 a racecourse was laid out on the expensively reclaimed land, replacing an earlier course located across the Laira at Crabtree. The site has since seen use as Plymouth city's refuse dump, although it has in more recent years been filled in and grassed over. John Parker III was also responsible for the south range of the stable block, constructed in the early 19th century.

A sporting estate

The deer park in the 18th century afforded ample opportunities for hunting and in 1773 Theresa wrote to her brother, 'Have shot an immense old stag in the park at Borringdon, we will eat tomorrow, prodigiously fat as it has not been hunted, is much better than Park venison.' The deer park fell into disuse by the 1820s but, with the coming of the railways in the second half of the 19th century and the subsequent growth of 'country house holidays', shooting parties frequently stayed at Saltram, particularly in the days of the 3rd and 4th Earls. The main house would be full of guests, beaters would be recruited from the estate staff, and great 'bags' of pheasants, woodcock, ducks and pigeon would be shot.

Above A shoot at Stag Lodge, 1894

Left A workers' cottage on the estate, c.1890

Industry and enterprise

It may seem that Saltram and its 4,000-acre estate could only have been built upon sound financial investment. But the truth is that successive generations of Parkers had to devise constant schemes to raise funds to support themselves.

Although the family ran the estate as a business, they expanded into other areas to improve their income. John Parker III constructed a shipbuilding yard for the Navy at Cattedown, where he also built commercial ships; his son developed a business in tallow and whale oil. However, not all their schemes were successful.

Ambitious engineering projects on the part of John Parker III had amassed debts of £258,000 by 1840. He had reclaimed estuary land at a cost of £15,000 to make the racecourse, and in 1824 he started work on a new toll bridge across the Laira. On completion in 1827, it was the second-largest iron structure in existence.

There was also investment in the slate quarries at Cann during this period, with the construction of a canal and tramway. Linked to the Plymouth and Dartmoor Tramway, they provided a much-improved transport connection to Plymouth. Although John Parker III negotiated reduced transport rates from the Plymouth and Dartmoor Tramway Company, the cost ultimately fell upon the Saltram purse. In order to address the financial situation, Edmund Parker, the 2nd Earl, sold off parts of the estate. He was also involved in the burgeoning china clay industry, investing money in the Lee Moor Clay Company. However, the enterprise lost thousands of pounds through mismanagement, and the company was wound up in 1889 by the 3rd Earl.

Below The construction of the cast-iron Laira Bridge in 1824 was paid for by the 1st Earl and severely depleted the estate's resources

Staffing the estate

A large part of the problem in maintaining Saltram as a going concern arose from the increasing costs of labour. Like many other country estates, Saltram relied on local people willing and able to work long hours for low wages. The coming of the railways in the mid-19th century and the drift to towns of young people looking for better-paid, less-demanding work led to a shortage of servants and staff.

Staff numbers were further depleted with the outbreak of the First World War in 1914, when many of Saltram's outdoor staff enrolled into the armed services. House staff were also more difficult to find after the War, and the resulting higher wages came to be even more of a drain on revenues. Despite this, the family managed to retain unusually high standards for the time, through the judicious sale of inherited property.

The war years

Part of the reason for the estate's survival into the 1930s was undoubtedly the care of a reduced but devoted house staff – eleven in all – but when the Second World War began, the 4th Earl, Edmund also known as 'B', and his younger brother Montagu, or 'Monty', were left with just two servants. Plymouth was a major target for the Luftwaffe; air-raid shelters were built in the park, and the large Venetian window in the Saloon was bricked up to protect it from the Blitz. Saltram did not escape the bombing and its home farm was badly damaged during a raid. During the preparations for D-Day, the American army set up a large camp at Merafield Lodge. The woods provided excellent camouflage for vehicles and equipment – a tank inspection pit from this era can still be seen in the garden.

Guaranteeing the future

The damage done to Saltram during the war years, coupled with the lack of staff to help manage the house and a shortage of materials to make repairs, left the estate in poor shape, despite the best efforts of the family. When the 4th Earl died in 1951, and his bachelor brother Monty succeeded him aged 73, it was apparent that death duties would take a great toll on the estate and radical plans had to be made. So in 1957, the estate was transferred to the National Trust and Saltram's survival was ensured.

Left During the Second World War the park was occupied by the American army

Below Saltram's future was secured when the estate was transferred to the National Trust in 1957

Surviving and sustaining

'Such has been the outward spread of Plymouth that Saltram is no longer an adornment of its surrounding countryside, more a desperately precious stretch of park amid the enveloping suburb.'

So wrote Simon Jenkins in *England's Thousand Best Houses*. It is perhaps remarkable that Saltram has survived at all, given its location so close to the thriving city of Plymouth. Although the 4,000 acres originally owned by the family have long since been sold and developed, a core 500 acres of park and woodland, the house and its contents are still

intact and open to the public. Nowadays, the estate has more than 750,000 visitors a year, providing the local and wider community with an 'open-air sitting room'. Visitors range from dog walkers to joggers, 'twitchers' to art historians, and picnicking families to cyclists using the Sustrans National Cycle Route 27.

But Saltram is not 'set in aspic'. Thanks to the commitment of the National Trust's expert staff and 200 volunteers, it is constantly being improved and upgraded, researched and conserved. In previous years, some items from the collection at Saltram had been lent to other less well-furnished Trust properties. However this policy has now been reversed and Saltram is recalling some of these objects.

Above Walkers along the beach at Saltram with the city of Plymouth just across the water

Left Joggers running on the drive

Opposite Cattle are still grazed on the estate

Wildlife on view

Interesting birdlife still inhabits the Saltram estate, but modern pastimes consist of observing them rather than potting them with guns. Because of its unique position, Saltram is a magnet for twitchers who use the hides overlooking the tidal estuary to watch numerous wading birds. At Blaxton Meadow the managed retreat is recreating a salt marsh habitat, which also provides a welcoming environment for the birds. The scheme is the result of a successful partnership between the Environment Agency, Natural England and the National Trust.

Saltram provides a haven for many varieties of endangered and protected wildlife. Four species of bats are known to roost on the estate; brown long-eared bats have been discovered in the roof of the Orangery, and greater and lesser horseshoes, and pipistrelles are found in various buildings. Bat colonies rely on suitable roost sites and the ready availability of insects, including dung beetles. The pastoral landscape at Saltram provides a suitable supply of dung, and is the perfect habitat.

The importance of parkland

The parkland has been under conservation management in the form of Countryside Stewardship (now Higher Level Scheme) for a number of years, with arable land and improved grassland restored to unfertilised permanent pasture. Most of the parkland is permanent pasture, while 108 acres are woodland managed under a Woodland Grant scheme.

The land has been included by English Heritage on their National Historic Parkland Register. The estate offers an important habitat resource; rare invertebrates are supported by the ancient trees, and rich lichen communities are testimony to the relatively unpolluted atmosphere. The trees also provide bat roosts and dwellings for hole-nesting birds.

As a rare survival of an 18th-century country estate, and one precariously perched on a city's edge, Saltram is an important resource for local residents. It is also a haven for diverse populations of flora and fauna, supported by sustainable farming practices, which add to the richness and variety of the estate.

The Garden

The garden at Saltram contains many fine specimen trees and shrubs, and notable examples from New Zealand and Chile. They thrive in the comparatively mild climate of the Plym Estuary, some 30 metres above sea level.

Hydrangea Paniculata with Sellick 1895 G Mong.

The garden's location on an exposed ridge means it is often buffeted by winds and can suffer from drought. The soil is shallow, underlain with shillet (a gravel of crushed shale) and is neutral to acid. In order to improve fertility and water retention, staff and volunteers add copious quantities of organic matter by mulching and incorporating more when planting.

At regular intervals of about a century, Saltram's magnificent woodland seems to be redesigned by nature. In 1799 severe storms caused great damage, and in March 1891 'The Great Blizzard' hit the West Country and blew down 400 trees at Saltram. 'It will take years to repair the damage,' Albert, the 3rd Earl, noted gloomily in his records. In 1990, 50 trees were lost in the garden and almost 1,000 were lost in the park.

Albert Parker's garden

The garden as it now appears was mostly created in the late 19th century by the 3rd Earl. Originally it was an 18th-century landscape which developed into a plantsman's garden when, in 1876, the 3rd Earl married Margaret Holford, whose father founded what is now Westonbirt Arboretum. The couple returned to Saltram in 1884 (it had been leased out to a Mr Hartmann by the 2nd Earl) and after tackling the neglect of the buildings, and planting a Lime Avenue to provide much-needed shelter, the 3rd Earl concentrated on the gardens, as a series of detailed planting books testify. His diaries record the major works in the garden, and list the many rare plants purchased, their planting location and their eventual fate: initially, there was a high failure rate, as British gardeners were unfamiliar with their needs and habits.

Opposite Sellick the gardener with a magnificent *Hydrangea paniculata*, taken in 1895

Growing the collection

The proximity of Plymouth, a major port, stimulated wealthy landowners' interest in collecting interesting and exotic plants brought back from long sea voyages to the New World. In the case of Saltram, rare and tender plants and less common trees were bought from specialist nurseries such as Veitches of Exeter, one of the most important dynasties of Victorian nurserymen, and Jeffreys of Cirencester. Many other plants came from Albert's father-in-law, R.S. Holford. Westonbirt also dispatched vast quantities of cut flowers by rail to Saltram, three times a week, to decorate the house.

However the 3rd Earl was himself prey to other, less scrupulous plant collectors: in 1888 he wrote to the local paper noting that, although he liked to leave Saltram woods open to the general public, quantities of both wild and naturalised plants were frequently stolen.

Clockwise from top left Sophora, Halesia, *Azalea luteum*, Camassia, *Michelia doltsopa*, *Embothrium coccinea*

A garden of many parts

No garden is static or fixed in time, and the grounds of Saltram have been changed by successive owners since the idealised landscape created in the 18th century by Nathaniel Richmond. Famous for its beautiful scents, the principal part of the garden lies beyond the Orangery.

Although renowned in the 18th and 19th centuries, the garden at Saltram was neglected during the Second World War and remained so until the arrival of the National Trust. Graham Stuart Thomas was gardens consultant to the National Trust, and he advised on the setting at Saltram. He recognised that the garden had a strong 18th-century character in the informal tradition, and was essentially a parkland with interesting vistas and specimen trees. He was careful to retain the later additions and improvements reflecting the enthusiasms of 19th-century plantsmen. 'GST', as he was known, ordered the improvement of lawns, the simplification of paths, the thickening of windbreaks and the care of shrubs by mulching and pruning.

Seasonal highlights

Spring bulb displays enliven many areas, especially the breath-taking stretch of nearly 300 metres of old varieties of narcissus beneath the Lime Avenue, followed later by *Cyclamen hederaefolium* – at their best between August and November. There are drifts of wild flowers in many areas during spring and summer, and behind the Orange Grove a good colony of Southern Marsh Orchids is developing.

Along North Path and Middle Glade and bordering a sunny area on the top lawn is a great variety of predominately evergreen trees and shrubs providing a good backbone of shelter, whilst giving structure and a backcloth to many flowering shrubs.

A mixed border near the Chapel, designed by GST, is at its best from June onwards. It features mixed plantings of roses, flowering shrubs and herbaceous plants. Colour is planned throughout the summer months, following on from the spring displays of camellias, rhododendrons and other early shrubs. It is in a very sheltered location and recent plantings have capitalised on this, including exotics such as bananas, echiums and ginger lilies. Records show that a cyclad, *Cycas revoluta*, was here in the 1920s, so one was re-introduced in 2002.

Above A carpet of daffodils in springtime in the Lime Avenue

Opposite left *Rhododendron x loderi* 'King George'

Opposite right An ornamental urn on the Melancholy Walk that leads to the grave of a beloved family pet

Original features

A cattle byre was altered in 1776 and designated a chapel on the initiative of Anne Robinson, possibly as a memorial to her sister Theresa. Lord Grantham was consulted and commented to his brother-in-law in October 1776, 'I approve much of the Plans and Elevations of your Chapel, which will be very handsome indeed.' It was restored by the National Trust in the 1970s.

Melancholy Walk is one of the oldest surviving paths in the garden, originally being a part of the 'Green Ride' leading to Saltram Point. It now takes you to the Castle. A mown grass path ornamented with stone columns and urns, it is at its best in the spring, with drifts of bluebells.

Fanny's Bower, previously known as the Temple of Jupiter, was renamed in honour of the novelist Fanny Burney (see page 7), who had accompanied the visit of King George III and his family in 1789, and was much taken with Saltram Wood, 'which abounds in seats of all sorts'.

The Orangery
The Orange Grove

The Orangery

The Orangery was built in 1773. In a letter from Theresa Parker to her brother she wrote that the Orangery was 'Stockman's improvement of a plan he saw of Mr Richmond's'. So while the concept and Neo-classical façade may well have been Nathaniel Richmond's, the final execution was down to the estate carpenter, Henry Stockman.

Records show that orange trees had been bought in 1771, and in 1782 the Orange Grove was created behind the Chapel as a summer location for the trees. Theresa Parker had high hopes for what they might cultivate here, noting that it was '…so warm a situation that we mean to plant all sorts of curious shrubs, myrtles we are sure will grow and geraniums we mean to try'.

Traditionally the citrus collection was put out for the summer on Oak Apple Day (22 May) and put away for the winter on Tavistock Goose Fair Day (the second Wednesday in October). More recently it has not been unusual to put them out in April and return them in November, depending on the weather.

The front part of the Orangery burnt down in 1932; it was restored by the National Trust in 1961. New orange trees were imported from Italy and placed in rectangular tubs based on the design of an old slate tub now in the Tudor Courtyard (see page 55). A modern fountain was installed in memory of the Hon. Brigadier Robin Parker, the last member of the family to live at Saltram, who died in 1999.

The Orange Grove

This area was created to accommodate the orange trees in their pots during summer, and dates from 1782. In 1886, the surrounding laurels were cut back and exotic plants from the Scilly Isles were planted. In 1892 a fountain was installed in the central pond, and a black walnut tree was planted at the north edge. This area of the garden has the feel of the Mediterranean: in good weather the feeling of enclosure makes it feel warmer still and the types of plants that grow here complete the effect.

Above **The Neo-classical façade of the Orangery**

Opposite **The Orange Grove dates from 1782**

The Castle

The Serpentine Walk

Landscape gardens of the 18th century were designed with recreation in mind, offering dramatic vistas often punctuated with small structures to amuse the visitor and to hint at the cultural tastes of the landowner. Robert Adam was commissioned to design a small folly – a cottage in the castle style – for the garden at Saltram. No trace of it survives if, indeed, it was ever built. The Castle, a whimsical octagonal summerhouse with an earlier cellar beneath, is in the romantic Gothick style. The interior is decorated in plasterwork, echoing the interiors of the house. In 1771 Theresa Parker wrote that 'something must be done upon that spot' to take advantage of the view over the estate and towards the sea.

The Serpentine Walk is a recent development, dating from 2003, lying on open ground sloping to the south. There are pastoral views to the south east, giving something of the flavour of the 18th-century landscape style, lost from other areas where views have been obscured by evergreen planting to reduce the effects of noise pollution and urban development.

There is a tank inspection pit in this area, built by the American troops stationed at Saltram in the Second World War, now surrounded by a hedge of *Osmanthus heterophyllus*, which flowers during the early winter.

Above **The Serpentine Walk**

Left **The Castle**

Specimen trees

The garden of Saltram is justifiably famous for its impressive specimens of rare and ancient trees. At the head of the Lime Avenue is a magnificent English oak, which is believed to be 700 years old. There are a number of impressive pines, mostly *Pinus radiata*, the Monterey pine. A couple of large, characterful sweet chestnuts, *Castanea sativa*, are frequently commented upon, especially the one near the Orangery. A large cork oak, *Quercus suber*, from Southern Europe is nearby, to the right of the path leading to the Orange Grove. Opposite this is a young Handkerchief or Dove Tree, *Davidia involucrata*, which is becoming a handsome specimen.

Sequoia sempervirens and *Sequoia wellingtonia* (Giant Redwoods) thrive on site, as do magnolias and cornus (Asian dogwoods). Less unusual but adding to the diversity of trees in the garden, is an avenue of parallel-planted holmoaks (*Quercus ilex*) underplanted with snowdrops.

Other species of note include the tulip trees, *Liriodendron tulipfera*: a huge tree stands near the eastern boundary of the garden, whilst a younger specimen on the main lawn is admired for its autumn colour. Acers also provide good autumnal shades.

Many areas of the garden are reminiscent of the arboretum at Westonbirt, which later generations of the Parker family also owned.

Above **Flowers of the Handkerchief Tree** (*Davidia involucrata*)

Tour of the House

Complete with its original décor, plasterwork and furnishings, Saltram is one of Britain's best-preserved Georgian houses. Originally a Tudor manor, the house has been altered over the centuries to fit the needs and tastes of its owners.

The south front is the main façade of the mid-18th-century house. The central pediment bears the family coat of arms, modelled in Coade stone in 1812, with the motto *Fideli certa merces* – 'Certain is the reward of the faithful'. When John Parker III became the 1st Earl of Morley in 1815, a coronet was added to the motif. The porch was designed by John Foulston in 1820; the Doric portico and anthemion (honeysuckle) motifs above the doors and the first-floor window are in the Greek Revival style.

The approach

Elegant and ordered, the exterior is Palladian in style. It has been rendered, a traditional technique often used when a cladding of cut stone would have been too expensive. The light colours and style of the façade recall the Mediterranean architecture of the ancient world.

The path to the house takes the visitor to the south entrance and offers an impressive view of the east front on the way. This was built during the mid-18th century, and its Palladian austerity belies the highly decorated interiors. Three storeys high, with two pedimented wings, the façade is symmetrical, hinging on the Venetian-style window in the centre of the ground floor, which leads into the Saloon. In fact, the wing to the left of the centre contains false windows to provide symmetry, which usefully allows extra wall space inside for hanging paintings.

The Entrance Hall

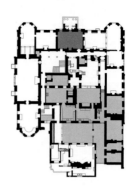

On entering Saltram the initial impression of elegance and ordered restraint is enhanced by the sophistication of its decoration. The magnificence of this space is intentionally stirring but is only a taste of what is to come.

To welcome visitors, the ceiling bears a large rococo plasterwork figure of Mercury, the god of good fortune, wealth and roads. To the weary traveller in an era before metalled roads and pneumatic tyres, this would have been a suitably benign and ironic reference to his journey.

Above each of the four doors leading out of the Entrance Hall are representations of the four elements: earth (Triumph of Venus), air (Astronomy), fire (Vulcan's forge) and water (a dolphin).

Sparse in furniture, the Entrance Hall served as a transition between the external world and the domestic interior. Furniture is primarily functional, though of very high quality.

Paintings

The Entrance Hall contains portraits of two of the key figures who created or transformed Saltram: the Thomas Hudson portrait of John Parker II, the 1st Lord Boringdon, depicts the man who commissioned Robert Adam to improve the interior of Saltram after he inherited the estate in 1768; on the other side of the entrance is a portrait inscribed as being his mother Lady Catherine, whose marriage into the Parker family provided the money for the major redevelopment of Saltram in the 1740s. However, some believe this to be his first wife, Frances Hort.

Left The plasterwork figure of Mercury on the Entrance Hall ceiling

Right Looking through the door in the Entrance Hall to the Red Room and Red Velvet Drawing Room

Sculpture

A fine sculpture, dated 1806, by the premier practitioner of the age, Joseph Nollekens, depicts John, the 1st Earl of Morley. The other busts, by unknown sculptors, depict the rather more idealised figures of Cicero, Apollo and Venus.

A 17th-century plasterwork overmantel, showing a king making a sacrifice, was given a rococo-style frame in the 1740s. The painted stone chimneypiece by Thomas Carter the Elder bears a central tablet depicting Androcles and the lion. The marble bust is an 18th-century copy of an ancient original, believed to depict Emperor Nerva.

Furnishings

The Louis XIV Boulle style bracket clock has a movement mechanism by Etienne Le Noir and is as functional as the stick barometer by Thomas Jones. Handsome side tables bear variously 17th-century Dutch Delft or Chinese Ming Dynasty porcelain vases. Mahogany hall-chairs bear the 1st Earl's coat of arms.

Right A Louis XIV Boulle style bracket clock, *c.*1740, which has a movement mechanism by Etienne Le Noir

The Red Room

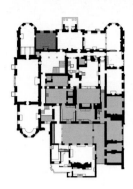

In contrast to the cool colours of the Entrance Hall, the Red Room is warmly and intricately decorated. Another room that underwent a change in function, its name is taken from the original wall coverings.

It was first created in the 1740s. The early Genoese silk velvet is still on the walls. The chimneypiece attributed to Sir Henry Cheere and the plaster ceiling depicting musical instruments in the form of a violin, lyre and recorder have not changed substantially for more than two and a half centuries. After probable use as a music room, it came to be used by the family for informal dining.

Family portraits

The most striking element in this room is its paintings, several of which depict family members, hung close together in the fashion of the time. The collection was begun by the first John Parker, on whose behalf the painter Sir Joshua Reynolds may have bought pictures when the artist was travelling in Italy between 1750 and 1752.

John Parker II added to the collection while making his own Grand Tour in 1764, and subsequently commissioned paintings from Angelica Kauffman and Reynolds.

A full hand-list of paintings is available in this room, but the highlights include *John Parker and his sister Theresa* as children painted in 1779 by Reynolds (see page 14), which hangs in prime position over the fireplace.

Opposite The Red Velvet Drawing Room

Left *Madonna and Child*, after Raphael, a 17th-century copy of the *Madonna della Sedia* (Red Room)

Right Closely hung paintings against the original red silk velvet walls of the Red Room

The Red Velvet Drawing Room

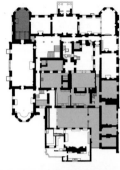

In 1770, Theresa, John Parker II's wife, '…with her usual taste orderd all the mouldings, & parts of the Capitals of the Columns to be Gilt, which makes the Room much chearfuller and handsomer…'.

Until Robert Adam created the Saloon in 1768, the Red Velvet Drawing Room was the main drawing room for the Parker family and their guests. Seeing this as the anteroom to his grand scheme, Adam later added details to the room, designing the pair of pier glasses and marble-topped console tables beyond the columns, to lead the way into his smart new Saloon.

Beyond the pillars a small piece of the original red silk velvet hangings survives on the wall near the entrance to the Saloon, but the rest of the room was redecorated with red flock in the 1950s. The walls are hung with paintings, representing a typical Grand Tour collection, including Dutch and Italian works.

A history of gambling
The piece of furniture that most draws the eye in this room is the giltwood side-table with a *scagliola* (inlaid stone) top decorated with a convincing *trompe l'oeil*. The craftsman is unknown, but with great virtuosity, he depicted the surface of a table apparently littered with abandoned playing cards, counters, and even a letter, bearing the date 2 May 1713, supposedly signed by John Pollexfen Junior, whose descendant married Lady Catherine's sister, Bridget.

The Saloon

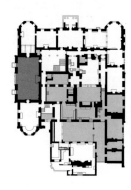

The Saloon at Saltram is generally believed to be one of Robert Adam's finest interiors. He was commissioned by John Parker II to create a magnificent formal room, and in 1768 he designed a scheme for this room and the next one, producing complete drawings for every aspect of the walls, chimneypieces and ceilings.

The designs for the Saloon and a library (now the Dining Room) were Adam's first commission for Saltram. The biggest structural change in the Saloon was Adam's bold design for a magnificent Venetian-style central window, with capitals copied from Diocletian's Palace at Split. An anthemion frieze matches the cornice, and the gilded door handles are illustrated in Adam's publication *Works in Architecture* (1779)

He designed four enormous pier glasses, each eight feet high, for the window wall; two were probably moved to sit either side of the fireplace in 1840.

Adam designed a chimneypiece for this room, but it was not used as one had already been installed by Thomas Carter the Younger.

Designed from the ceiling down

Adam's ceiling design is based on three ovals, each containing a lozenge shape and a roundel. The roundel paintings are by Antonio Zucchi, whose central paintings make subtle reference to John Parker II's passion for hunting. Zucchi also worked for Robert Adam on his London

masterpiece, Osterley Park, and he was later to marry the painter Angelica Kauffman.

The carpet measures 46 by 22 feet, and the design echoes the pattern in the ceiling. It was woven by Thomas Witty at Axminster in 1770 at a cost of £126. The movable furniture was designed to go around the walls without visually interrupting the complex pattern of the carpet.

Custom-made furniture

The furniture commissioned for this setting includes a magnificent giltwood suite of eighteen chairs and two sofas attributed to Thomas Chippendale. The purchase came to £225, according to the account books.

The pair of giltwood side tables were probably designed by Adam, and Joseph Perfetti made the table frames at a cost of £41 1s 0d. The table tops are made of inlaid marble and came from Florence.

The set of four six-branch candelabra, made of bluejohn (Derbyshire feldspar) and ormolu, were made by Matthew Boulton in 1772 and are similar to a set made for George III.

The chandeliers were added in the early 19th century. A pale blue damask fabric covered the walls at a cost of £300. The fabric on the walls today dates from 1950.

Right Robert Adam's ceiling designs from 1765 for the Saloon

The best of the best

Adam's decorative scheme included overmantel and overdoor paintings, but the Parkers also wanted to use the room to show the highlights of their art collection. The four key portraits by Sir Joshua Reynolds include his touching depiction of Theresa Parker. Lady Theresa died within three years of the completion of this painting, and Reynolds, a family friend, wrote, 'Her amiable disposition, her softness and gentleness of manners, endeared her to every one that had the happiness of knowing her.'

A full hand-list of paintings is available, but of particular note is the early copy of Titian's *The Andrians* that hangs over the fireplace. The magnificent frame was probably designed by Adam and made by Chippendale.

Other decorative elements include pieces of Japanese Imari porcelain dating from the late 17th century, and early 18th-century bronzes on the mantelpiece by Giacomo and Giovanni Zoffolli.

Above **The Saloon**

East Corridor

At the staircase end of the East Corridor is a set of eight *grisaille* (in greyish tints) paintings of classical statuary by Louis Gabriel Blanchet (1705–72). Pictured is a hermaphrodite from the Villa Borghese, dated 1765. The Villa Borghese was the suburban residence of Scipione Borghese, Italian Cardinal and art collector, and was located of the outskirts of Rome.

Further along are some of Adam's drawings for the Saloon; the design for a great house dedicated to Lady Catherine Parker; and a set of ten early 19th-century gouache figures.

The Dining Room

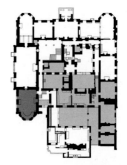

This room was originally designed by Robert Adam as a library, in 1768–70. A decade later John Parker II decided to relocate the dining room to make it more convenient to reach from the new kitchens that were built in 1778 after a fire damaged the old ones.

Adam was engaged to make the changes and provided designs for many aspects of the room, from the chimneypiece (probably executed by Thomas Carter the Younger) to the cellarette or wine cooler under the side table.

Some structural changes were introduced during the conversion into a dining room. Two windows were blocked to make alcoves, and a sideboard was designed for the bay to provide visual continuity while creating an efficient servery. The alcoves contain a pair of Etruscan plaster urns, purchased in 1770 for £50.

The design of the ceiling was by Adam, with plasterwork by Joseph Rose, who was paid £434 between 1770 and 1772 for his skilled craftsmanship in this room and the Saloon. The carpet pattern and colouring echo that of the ceiling, and the carpet was also supplied by Thomas Whitty of Axminster.

A 'moveable feast'

The Georgian mahogany dining table is usually laid for twelve diners using the family's Marseilles dinner service. Both the table and the set of oval-backed chairs would have been removed or placed around the walls when not in use.

A changing room

Traces of the room's original purpose still remain: on the fireplace wall there were two pairs of bookshelves, and the traces are still just visible under the current medallions.

The theme of learning and knowledge permeates the painted decoration: on the ceiling the four lunettes depict classical scenes. The medallion heads in the corners portray the classical thinkers Socrates, Zeno, Cicero and Thales of Miletus.

Over the doors are scenes from Greek antiquity based on discovery and education. The first paintings were by Antonio Zucchi, and when the bookcases were removed the same artist provided six landscapes to complement the landscape overmantel by Zuccarelli.

Multiple functions

A pair of green vases and pedestals, designed by Robert Adam and painted with vignettes attributed to Angelica Kauffman, served as wine coolers. But the design addressed matters practical as well as aesthetic. In each supporting plinth is a discreet cupboard, one holding a plate warmer and the other concealing a chamberpot.

Above This medallion depicting the classical writer Cicero recalls the Dining Room's original function

Opposite The Georgian mahogany dining table is usually laid for twelve

The Kitchen

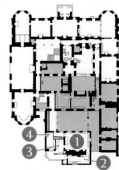

In 1778 a fire at the north end of Saltram House destroyed the laundry and brewhouse. A new kitchen complex was built, free-standing so as to minimise the risk of further fires and contain cooking smells.

1 The Kitchen

The Kitchen was remodelled in 1913 and remained in everyday use until the death of the 5th Earl in 1962. Several staff including French chefs were required to run the kitchen, to feed the family and their guests, and to provide less sophisticated fare for their fellow-servants, and it was the engine room of the servants' wing. The great hearth contains an open range from about 1810, and has roasting spits which were turned by the heat generated by the fire. A fan located inside the chimney would start to turn as the heat rose, drawing away excess heat and any smoke. The massive cast-iron closed range in the middle of the kitchen dates from 1885 and was made by Flavel & Co of Leamington. It held two ovens and was run on coal, and was the main source of hot water for the house. To avoid the need to put in a separate chimney, an underfloor flue lead to the back of the great hearth, and the updraught carried away the smoke.

Among the many implements and kitchen utensils, there is a magnificent copper *batterie de cuisine* – 600 items from giant stockpots and pans, jugs and ornate jelly moulds, all lined with tin.

'…immense & in the utmost order of neatness, the Kitchen with all its Appendent offices is a most complete thing…'

The Rev Thomas Talbot, the Countess's brother, writing in 1811

Above The Kitchen with its centrally placed stove

Right The iron lantern suspended from the ceiling of the Kitchen

The Scullery
The Pantry
The Butchery

2 The Scullery

The Scullery was used for washing up the prodigious amounts of dirty dishes and glasses generated when the family was in residence, and is fitted with two late 19th-century sinks, one of porcelain for washing fine china, the other of copper for washing pots and pans. Vegetables were prepared in the Scullery. In the days before plumbing, water would be poured out here for all washing purposes, and carried to distant bedrooms and dressing rooms several times a day. The white cans were for cold water, and the brown painted cans for hot.

3 The Pantry

The house would have been mostly self-sufficient in terms of everyday foodstuffs, and large quantities of bread and pastry would have been prepared in the Pantry – the flour bins still survive. One staple that had to be bought in was sugar, which was sold as a solid block, from which the cook would snip or pare off fragments. The sugar loaf in the Pantry would have weighed 15lbs.

4 The Butchery

A utilitarian room, the Butchery was fitted with a rack from which joints, game and sides of meat could be hung, a pallet for transporting larger carcasses, and chopping tables for meat preparation. The sinks were used for salting meat.

Right The view into the Pantry showing a towering block of sugar

The Staircase Hall

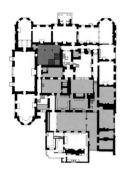

Full-height and well lit for the display of some fine paintings, the Staircase Hall dates from the 1740s. The central skylight has an iron frame and throws daylight into the hall. The plasterwork ceiling is in the Rococo style and was also installed in the mid-18th century.

The staircase is largely of mahogany with deal treads; the balusters are alternately fluted and spiral. In the time of John Parker II, the Staircase Hall opened into the Red Velvet Drawing Room and Red Room, as well as the Saloon and Entrance Hall, but two of the doors are now blocked.

Paintings

Today the Staircase Hall houses some of the most significant paintings at Saltram, many of them depicting classical themes. George Stubbs (1724–1806) is best known for his skill at painting animals, particularly horses, but an unusual work by him is entitled *The Fall of Phaethon*, 1777. It shows Apollo's son, Phaethon, losing control while driving the chariot of the sun, and being struck by a thunderbolt hurled by Jupiter to avert disaster.

Of the nine paintings by Angelica Kauffman, four reveal a familiarity with Greek mythology. Her most sensitive and appealing portrait depicts Sir Joshua Reynolds, and dates from 1767, when it was bought by John Parker II. Reynolds is pictured in 17th-century dress with a bust of Michelangelo, his artistic hero, and volumes of Johnson's *Idler*, Burke's *Sublime and the Beautiful*, and Goldsmith's *Traveller*. Reynolds was a friend of all three authors and at the centre of London literary life.

A portrait of Lady Catherine Parker on the ground floor is attributed to Michael Dahl. Lady Catherine was the second daughter of the 1st Earl Poulett and she married John Parker in 1725, bringing into the family a substantial fortune which paid for the renovations of Saltram in the 1740s.

The portrait on the landing of Vincenzo II Gonzaga, Duke of Mantua (1594–1627), was painted by Sir Peter Paul Rubens (1577–1640), and formerly belonged to King Charles I. The youngest son of Vincenzo I, the subject became a cardinal but renounced his position when it became known that he had married a much older widow.

Left The Staircase Hall

Opposite *The Fall of Phaethon*, by George Stubbs, 1777

The Chinese Dressing Room and Bedroom

This suite of rooms was always considered to offer the best apartments in the house and would have accommodated the most distinguished guests. In the 19th century they were decorated in blue and known as the Blue Bow Dressing Room and Bedroom.

1 The Chinese Dressing Room

The dressing room was where the gentleman of the house would submit to the ministrations of his valet or where a visiting lady's maid would sleep. The room contains handsome though largely unadorned furniture, mostly made of mahogany. There is a dwarf wardrobe, and an enclosed and fitted washstand with an adjustable toilet mirror.

The 18th-century medicine chest is well designed to make a compact and secure case, tough enough to withstand the rigours of travel before the coming of the railways. It contains a battery of lotions and potions, and even a device for making pills, as nobody of quality would travel without his own medicaments.

A taste for chinoiserie
China had a great tradition of decorative painting, but the country had no indigenous wallpaper industry. But, through European trade with the city of Canton and to feed the growing appetite in Europe for chinoiserie, decorative rolls of painted paper started to reach Britain in the 1690s. The pattern in the dressing room is known by the Dutch term 'lange Lyzen' ('tall women'), known to English customers as 'Long Elizas'. Unusually elongated figures have been painted by hand onto the mulberry paper. On close scrutiny it is evident that at some point birds and other shapes have been cut out of another paper and glued over gaps in the design, a technique also used in the making of scrap screens, an extremely popular hobby in the 19th century.

Above The Chinese Bedroom with a mahogany four-poster bed, possibly supplied by Thomas Chippendale

Left Glass bottles neatly racked in an 18th-century portable medicine chest

2 The Chinese Bedroom

From the late 18th century this room was called the Blue Bow, because of the bow windows. It has fulfilled various functions since its completion, being used at times as a bedroom, and as an informal sitting or dining room.

The wallpaper in this room was hand-painted on silk in China and imported by the East India Company, a trading enterprise which became enormously powerful throughout Asia. As a result of the Western demand for a wide variety of oriental imports, some confusion was inevitable; Chinese wallpaper was often called 'India paper'.

The very obvious oriental theme in the dressing room is enhanced by Chinese and Japanese ceramics; a pair of Imari figures of Japanese women date from about 1700, and a porcelain *famille rose* jug depicting an emperor and his court dates from the late 18th century.

The mahogany four-poster bed dates from about 1760, and may have come from the workshop of Thomas Chippendale. The oriental taste is evident in the design of the four 'Chinese Chippendale' chairs, with their pagoda-shaped cresting rails. Mahogany hanging shelves in a co-ordinating style are designed to display porcelain, and are complemented by a group of mid-18th century Chinese mirror paintings, with contemporary English giltwood frames carved in the Rococo style.

Scenes of industry

This paper is of the type known as 'factory paper', because it typically shows everyday activities and trades being carried on in the cities where it was made, usually the bustling trading port of Canton, now known as Guangzhou. The scenes portrayed here revolve around the growing, curing and packing of tea: pictured are merchants and labourers treading tea leaves. Depictions of people, as in this case, were considered superior to wallcoverings showing birds and flowers and consequently were more expensive.

The Sitting Room

This room was originally a small sitting room for the use of the chatelaine, or mistress of the house. It has a service door that opens on to the Staircase Hall for ease of access by the servants. Today the room offers visitors the opportunity to sit and to browse albums of family photographs.

Here also are portraits of some of the key people in Saltram's history: John Parker, who purchased Saltram in 1712; the first three Earls and Countesses of Morley; estate carpenter and amateur architect Henry Stockman; and a sensitive portrait by an unknown hand of Anne Robinson, the beloved 'Aunt Nanny' (see page 15).

Above A Parker family photograph taken in 1848

Monty (top right) was evidently a keen amateur photographer: his father the 3rd Earl in the Entrance Hall (bottom right) and the Staircase Hall (bottom left) in 1889

Lady Morley's Bedroom
The Green Dressing Room

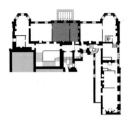
Lady Morley's Bedroom

This central bedroom, with access to the roof over the porch, is shown as if the mistress of the house has just left.

There are some fine pieces of furniture here, including one of the best in Saltram's collection. The very fine Louis XVI écritoire (writing desk) by Maurice-Bernard Evald (or Ewalde) was made in Paris between 1770 and 1774. Evald's work is very rare due to the short lifetime of his workshop. The two inlaid vases of flowers on the doors are after engravings by the French designer Maurice Jacques who worked at the Gobelins manufactory.

The Green Dressing Room

This room was given its name because of the colour of the wallpaper, and in the 19th century it was probably used by Lady Morley as her dressing room. In the days before reliable plumbing, all hot and cold water had to be carried in cans or jugs by servants from the Scullery, the water then laboriously removed.

However for the occupant, it would have been rather cosy, with a fire burning in the grate and gas lamps giving a soft glow. On the walls are a number of engravings, some of them depicting portraits by Sir Joshua Reynolds, which were once in the hands of the Parker family.

Bottom left This 18th-century writing desk is a rare example from the workshop of Maurice-Bernard Evald

Bottom right *David Garrick* (1717–79) *between 'Tragedy' and 'Comedy'* (after Sir Joshua Reynolds); by Edward Fisher (Green Dressing Room)

Lord Morley's Bedroom
The Study
The Map Room

1 Lord Morley's Bedroom

John Parker II, whose racing colours were green with a black cap, had a great interest in horseracing, which is highlighted in this room. There are two paintings here by John Nost Sartorius (1759–1828) of prize-winning horses from Lord Morley's stables: 'Saltram' won the 1783 Derby (only the third time it had been run) and was later bought by William Lightfoot of Virginia in 1799, but died three years later; 'Anvil' made his owner huge amounts of money before he was sold to the Prince of Wales in 1784. After an illustrious racing career, 'Anvil' was eventually retired to stud at Aston Linton in Buckinghamshire.

2 The Study

This room was used by Albert Edmund Parker, the 3rd Earl as a study while he was an MP.

The Chinese wallpaper in this room is extremely rare; it was hung in the 1750s and was hand-painted as a sequence of vertical panels, depicting human figures. Some are set in idyllic landscapes, with willowy beauties, balustraded gardens and a Western sense of perspective; others depict heroic warriors against a more traditional two-dimensional background.

The oriental theme continues in the seven Chinese Chippendale elbow chairs and the fine *blanc-de-Chine* porcelain figure of the Goddess Kuan Yin, the Maternal on the mantelpiece.

On the central table is a Florentine casket that belonged to the Earl's sister, Lady Katherine Parker, and is inset with specimen marbles. Lady Katherine, who died in 1910, did much research into the history of her illustrious family.

3 The Map Room

As its name suggests this room once housed the family's extensive collection of estate and other maps.

The room has recently been restored as a space where various conservation and other activities can be demonstrated in front of visitors, and where temporary exhibitions may be held.

Left The Parkers' Derby-winning racehorse 'Saltram'; by John Nost Sartorius, 1783 (Lord Morley's Bedroom)

Opposite The Study is hung with extremely rare Chinese wallpaper

The Western Apartments

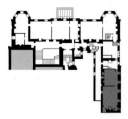

The Western Apartments house the paintings thought to be the work of Frances Talbot, second wife of the 1st Earl of Morley.

Frances Talbot was drawn to painting from a young age. Family tradition has it that she went to France as a young woman to train as a painter. That was in 1802. Much later, after 1840 when she was widowed, she spent a lot of time painting in oils and watercolour. Her subjects varied; she copied Old Masters and picturesque Continental views after paintings by contemporary artists such as William Callow and David Roberts.

In 1809 she was concerned about her nephew and niece's artistic education and she urged her sister-in-law to 'get a set of heads taken from Raphael's cartoons … they are the very finest and best things they could copy … let them draw them again and again'.

The Large and Small Drawing Rooms

Formerly bedrooms, these rooms are now used as galleries to show the work of the gifted Frances Talbot and include a copy of a portrait by Thomas Phillips, showing Frances when she was 20 years old. She is depicted as Lavinia, the heroine of *Autumn*, a poem by James Thomson (1700–48), wearing green (her favourite colour) and holding a sheaf of corn.

Right *Miss Talbot*; by
Thomas Phillips, 1802

The West Passage
The West and South Corridors
The Tudor Courtyard

The West Passage

This wide passage links the guest rooms to the service areas of the house, and also returns to the main staircases.

Shown here are some very fine prints including an early set of seven engravings after the famous cartoons of the *Acts of the Apostles* by Raphael, now in the Victoria and Albert Museum; they are in their original chinoiserie lacquer frames with crown glass.

The passage leads to the spiralling White Staircase and past it to the Red Stairs Lobby and on to the Red Stairs, a secondary staircase by which the ground floor is reached.

The West and South Corridors

These ground-floor corridors are paved with flagstones and contain a variety of family portraits, an early estate map, views of the estate, some testimonials and showcases with collections of oriental and other porcelains.

The Tudor Courtyard

The West Corridor opens onto the Tudor Courtyard, a central well which would have been screened from the eyes of aristocratic visitors in the 18th century. The courtyard provides a fascinating insight into the slow, almost organic development of the house over the centuries.

The 17th-century Bagge Tower looms over the courtyard. The walls are studded with windows and doors from different eras, and there are visible scars where walls have been taken down and doorways bricked up.

Below The internal courtyard preserves fragments of Tudor Saltram and the tower built by the Bagge family in the 17th century

The Garden Room

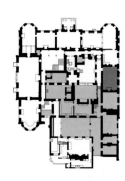

On the other side of the West Corridor is a room which has been used variously for playing billiards and as a study for the 4th Earl of Morley. Now known as the Garden Room, it shows a collection of paintings depicting Saltram in the late 18th and early 19th centuries.

William Tomkins (c.1732–92) was an itinerant painter of country estates and seven pictures by him survive at Saltram. Of particular interest is his rendition of *The Amphitheatre at Saltram*, 1770 (see page 19), which depicts John Parker II's private barge bringing a party to

Blaxton Quay while a salute is fired from cannon. The Amphitheatre was almost certainly built by John Parker I and still stands on the banks of the Laira, the estuary of the River Plym.

The two French hunting horns over the door were made in London, one by John Christopher Hofmaster and the other by Nicholas Winkings.

Above The Garden Room displays various paintings depicting 18th- and 19th-century Saltram

The Mirror Room

In the 18th century a staircase led from this room to the first floor, but that was removed and the room now sports hand-painted Chinese wallpaper depicting scenes from everyday life.

This is a much-changed room with exceptional Chinese wallpaper, which forms a perfect backdrop to the property's exceptional collection of Chinese mirror painting. Five of these have ornate mid-18th-century English giltwood frames in the Rococo style; the others are still in their original black and gold lacquer frames.

The fashion for chinoiserie in mid-18th century society was a counterbalance to the classical style; it reflected a more playful approach to the decorative arts, and was also a reflection of Britain's expansion of trade with the Far East. It is not uncommon to find 'Chinese' style decorations in otherwise Neo-classical mansions; great houses such as Kedleston and Osterley have collections of Chinese and Japanese ceramics and lacquerwork. The fashion for the oriental style informed English furniture makers too.

A set of mahogany chairs in this room are in the 'Chinese Chippendale' style, the furniture designer's response to public demand. A further two chairs, similar to those from the Chinese Chippendale Bedroom on the first floor, are made of padouk wood and have fretwork backs and pagoda-shaped cresting rails. Also here, in a large cabinet, are some of Saltram's fine collection of English and European porcelains. These include some rare pieces from William Cookworthy's Plymouth porcelain works, which only lasted from 1768 until 1770.

Left A close-up of the mantelpiece and ceramics, including an 18th-century Japanese Arita porcelain carp

Right A porcelain figure of a fisherman holding two fish with others stuffed in his shirt. It is by Chelsea and dates from *c*.1755–57

The Library

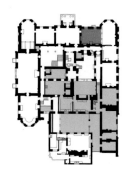

The Library

The Library was originally two rooms, a dining room and a drawing room. The dining room was relocated to the Adam-designed library in 1778. The drawing room continued to be used as such, hosting musical soirées and other entertainments until 1819, when the 1st Earl of Morley instructed local architect John Foulston to combine them and create a large library. Replacing the dividing wall with *scagliola* (imitation marble) columns, he created a magnificent space for the Earl's exceptional library of books.

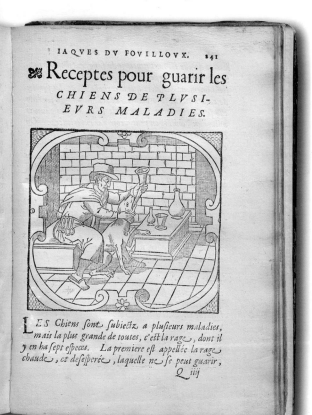

IAQVES DV FOVILLOVX.   241

❧ Receptes pour guarir les
CHIENS DE PLVSI-
EVRS MALADIES.

LES Chiens sont subiectz a plusieurs maladies, mais la plus grande de toutes, c'est la rage, dont il y en ha sept especes. La premiere est appellée la rage chaude, et desesperée, laquelle ne se peut guarir,
Q iiij

The collection

The white marble chimneypieces and overmantel mirrors were probably purchased on the family's visit to France in 1818. The cornices and pediments were added to the book presses in the early 20th century.

Many of the books were acquired during the 1st Earl's lifetime. He was particularly keen on collections of prints, which he and his wife collected and mounted in albums.

He also sought out unusual books reflecting his own interests; one of the earliest in the library is *La Venerie* by Jacques de Fouilloux, a French manual on hunting, published in Poitiers in 1564.

Left *La Venerie* by Jacques du Fouilloux, 1564, is a French manual on hunting. This page starts the chapter on curing dogs of illness

Right The *scagliola* columns replaced the dividing wall when the Library became one room

Opposite The 'Patent Metamorphic Library Chair' by Morgan and Sanders; Regency mahogany library steps fold up to form a sabre-leg armchair

Furnishings

The centrepiece of the room, the rare and beautiful writing desk was made around 1700 and is thought to be from the workshop of renowned French cabinetmaker Andre-Charles Boulle. It is overlaid with brass and shell and has multi-coloured inlays of mother-of-pearl, ivory and dyed woods. Representations of Asia, Europe, Africa and America adorn each corner. It is one of ten known pieces of furniture in this rare and distinctive style.

The Parker family believed that the desk was once the property of King Louis XIV of France. Records suggest that it came to Saltram in the 1750s through the Duchess of Marlborough.

Portraits by the president

The Library boasts a wide range of portraits of family, friends and influential contemporaries; likenesses in all media were considered appropriate to places of enlightenment and learning in the 19th century. Portraits also had the practical advantage of being relatively small and therefore easily hung between the bookshelves and ceiling.

Of the four portraits by Sir Joshua Reynolds, the picture of John Parker I (1703–68), who remodelled Saltram in the 1740s, is perhaps the most important. The neighbouring portrait, of Sir John Chichester, 5th Bt (1721–84) shows the head of an old North Devon family, who lived at Raleigh. In 1773, Theresa Parker dismissed Sir John as 'such a lump of wood'. However it is the picture of John Arscott (d.1788) by James Northcote, which is the most intriguing. Mr Arscott was the epitome of the old-fashioned country squire, and the last private gentleman to maintain a professional jester, Black John, whose specialities were swallowing mice and the bizarre sport of sparrow-mumbling.

Commissions by Kauffman

Angelica Kauffman's portrait of John Parker II, later 1st Lord Boringdon (1734/5–88) was painted while he was on his honeymoon Grand Tour with his first wife, Frances Hort. Here he has powdered hair, in contrast to the Reynolds portrait of him in the Red Room. At the same time he acquired a self-portrait by Angelica Kauffman showing the artist playing a guitar. Although it has been damaged, it remains an evocative and unusual work.

Left *John Parker II, later 1st Lord Boringdon*; by Angelica Kauffman, 1764

Below *Portrait of the artist*; by Angelica Kauffman